THE
MAY
BABY

THE
May
BABY

★

Noel Streatfeild

First published in 1959
This edition published in 2023 by Headline Home
an imprint of Headline Publishing Group

1

Cataloguing in Publication Data is available from the British Library

Hardback ISBN 978 1 0354 0847 4
eISBN 978 1 0354 0848 1

Typeset in 14.75/15pt Centaur MT Pro by Jouve (UK), Milton Keynes

Printed and bound in Great Britain by Clays Ltd, Elcograf S.p.A.

Headline's policy is to use papers that are natural, renewable and recyclable
products and made from wood grown in well-managed forests and other
controlled sources. The logging and manufacturing processes are expected
to conform to the environmental regulations of the country of origin.

HEADLINE PUBLISHING GROUP
An Hachette UK Company
Carmelite House
50 Victoria Embankment
London EC4Y 0DZ

www.headline.co.uk
www.hachette.co.uk

CONTENTS

PERHAPS the nicest month of the year in which to be born is May. The month of which Shakespeare wrote 'Love, whose month was ever May.'

The news has flown round, and all the questions have been asked. How are you? How is the baby? Is it a he or a she, what colour are its eyes, has it any hair, what did it weigh at birth? And now you are to have visitors, and the talking point is 'What shall I take her?'

Flowers have been pouring in on you, and May is a good month for flowers. Irises of all colours, and perhaps the most glorious of all spring blossom, the lilac, and of course tulips. But it can be possible if you are in a hospital or nursing home to have too many flowers, for there must come a time when even the sunniest-tempered nurse says, sweetly but meaningly, 'We're running out of vases, and I don't know what I'm going to put these in.'

Fruit is a welcome present, but May is a bad month for fruit. There are forced strawberries to be had, but they are usually very tasteless. Though not exactly fruit, there is of course asparagus, but unless you are at home asparagus is out, for it is seldom looked upon favourably by the cook of a hospital or nursing home. So that means falling back on grapes, and too many grapes can be a bore for there comes a time when everybody is surfeited with them, and you can't give them away.

For the rich something for the mother to wear is nice, but most mothers have friends and relations who are not rich, and far from being able to bring something pretty for the mother to wear, come to the bedside saying, 'Do you think this hat looks all right again this year? I really can't go on wearing my winter ones, but I can't afford anything new.'

Of course there are always presents for baby. These can vary from rattles to premium bonds, and if the latter very nice too. But those hurrying to the bassinet with premium bonds can be reckoned on a few fingers, and neither mother nor baby really want rattles, and few are the friends and relations who have had the strength of mind to keep the baby clothes they have made or bought until the baby has arrived. So probably it won't be a present for baby.

It is years of wondering what to bring to mother and baby that has resulted in this book. Two things stand out in all conversations round the bassinet, first that no other topic

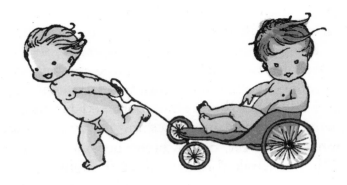

but baby is really interesting to the mother, and secondly, however leisured the mother may look to the visitor, she has in fact no leisure at all. What with feeding baby, being washed and tidied, doing exercises and resting, she scarcely has time to open a book. The answer clearly is a short book full of snippets, all relating to the May baby.

First, names come to the mind. Of course most parents know exactly what they are going to call the baby, whether a he or she arrives. But there are always waverers, who balance like trapeze artists between names, sometimes swaying towards one and sometimes towards another. For such, the list in this book may be of assistance if only that it makes them say, 'Well, I won't call baby any of those.'

It is difficult not to be interested in the signs of the zodiac, for it is fascinating to speculate on the supposed attributes your baby should have. But before you judge whether you believe what is written or not, turn to the list of the famous born in May. Were Florence Nightingale and Edward Lear really the same sort of people? And how surprising to find Elizabeth Fry sharing a birthday with Philip the Second of Spain. And who shares your baby's birthday?

It is hoped, having studied all the information about May babies collected here for your amusement, that you are satisfied that your baby was born in a good month.

NAMES
for the
MAY
BABY

MAY is the name which jumps to the mind for a May baby girl. It is a 19th century shortened version of *Margaret* which means 'pearl'. Sometimes it is spelt *Mai* or *Mae*.

May is the fifth month; *Quentin* or *Quintin* mean 'fifth', and the birth stone is an emerald, so how about *Emerald* or *Esmeralda* for a girl?

In old English poems we read about the 'merrie' month of May; there are several names with cheerful meanings, if *Gay* or *Joy* are too simple a choice. *Beatrice, Beatrix* and *Venetia* mean 'bringer of joy', and *Charmian* 'a little joy'. *Evangeline* is the 'bearer of good tidings,' *Letitia* and *Lettice* mean 'gladness', *Naomi* 'pleasant'. *Hilary* (which is equally suitable for a boy or girl) means 'cheerful'. *Jocelyn, Josceline* and *Joceline* for a girl, and

Jocelin or *Joscelin* for a boy, all mean 'merry'. *Eden* means 'delight', *Felix* 'happy', *Felicia* and *Felicity* mean 'happiness'. The modern form of *Abigail*, which is charming though very old-world, is *Gail* or *Gale*, and means 'father rejoiced'. *Gavin* means 'hawk of the month of May'.

If you believe that names influence people, and since May is a fortunate month, you might consider some names connected with fame. *Cuthbert* means 'famous splendour', *Aylmer* and *Elmer* 'nobly famous', *Luther* 'famous warrior', *Mervin* and *Mervyn* 'famous friend', *Roderic* or *Roderick* 'famous ruler', *Roger* means 'spear of fame', *Orlando, Roland* and *Rowland* mean 'fame of the land', *Rolf* and *Rollo* 'wolf-fame'. *Howell* means 'eminent', and *Magnus* 'great'. For girls there are fewer names to choose from. *Gloria, Roma* and *Romola* mean 'fame', *Heloisa* and *Heloise* mean 'famous holiness', and *Maxine* 'greatness'.

There are more festivals to do with the 1st of May than almost any other day in the calendar. The Romans called May after Maia mother of Mercury, messenger of their gods. Angels are God's messengers, and this is what *Angel* means, and so do *Angelica* and *Angelina*. *Malachi* means 'my messenger'. The Romans dedicated the 1st of May to Flora, their goddess of flowers. *Flora* and *Fleur* mean 'flower', and *Anthea* 'flowery'. *Carmel* and *Carmen* mean 'garden'.

Florence means 'blooming'. While considering flowery names how about *Deborah* and *Melissa* which both mean a 'bee', or *Pamela* 'all honey'?

In mediaeval times May-Day was often celebrated with plays, one of which told the legend of Robin Hood, so how about *Robin* for a boy? It is a diminutive of *Robert* which means 'bright fame', as do *Rupert* and *Roberta*. Allan-a-dale is another, character in the play, so how about *Allan, Alan* or *Allen*, all of which mean 'harmony', or Maid Marian? *Marian* means 'wished-for child'. Morris

dancing too, was part of the old celebrations on May the first. *Morris* or *Maurice* means 'moor'.

Today, Labour Day is celebrated on May the first, so here are some names which bring work into their meanings. *Amery, Emery* and *Meyrick* mean 'work-ruler'. *Lance* and *Lancelot* 'boy-servant'. *Rodney* 'road-servant'. *Gillespie* 'servant of a bishop'. *Ida* means 'labour', and *Millicent* 'work-strong'. Three names are particularly suitable for Labour Day, they are *Fulke* which means 'one of the people', and

Nicholas and *Nicol* which mean 'victory of the people'.

May is not as rich in saints' days as some of the other months. The apostle which legend

assigns to the month is *Bartholomew*, which means 'abounding in furrows.'

The first day of May is shared by St Philip and St James. *Philip* means 'horse-lover', and so does *Philippa*. *James* comes from *Jacob*, 'supplanter', and so do *Hamish, Jacques, Jamie* and *Shamus*, and for girls *Jacqueline* and *Jacquetta*, have the same meaning. The 19th of

May is the day of St Dunstan. *Dunstan* means 'hill stone'.

The 26th of May is St Augustine's day, he was Archbishop of Canterbury. *Augustin, Augustus,*

Austin, Bastian and *Sebastian* mean 'venerable', for a girl *Augusta* has the same meaning. *Alda* means 'old', and so do *Aldo* and *Aldous. Priscilla* means 'ancient'.

The sign of the zodiac for the last part of May is Gemini, the Twins. *Thomas* means 'twin', and *Mace* is a shortened form of it, or for a girl the old-fashioned *Thomasina.*

But for a truly May name, how about *Buttercup* for a baby girl? It is in May that the meadows become sheets of gold, and *Buttercup* is a delicious name; it is strange it is not more often used.

GIFTS
for the
MAY
BABY

15

IF a godparent or other well-wisher would like to give the baby a piece of jewellery, the right stone for May is the emerald. Mothers of May babies will probably sigh and wish that emeralds were not as expensive as they are beautiful, for not many babies will receive such an opulent present. The birth stone for each month in the year has a meaning, and the emerald is the symbol of love success. Here is an extract from a book which was published in 1569, in the time of the first Elizabeth, called *Certaine Secrete Wonders of Nature*, which gives interesting information to do with emeralds.

'They write that it abhorres all uncleane and filthie livers, and is a special friend to chastitie ... Sana Verola affirmeth that if it be layed to the thighe of a woman feeling the paine of childe bearing, it procures deliverie.'

The charming old custom of arranging flowers or blossom in a vase or bunch so that it brings a message is almost forgotten today. But if your baby should receive a posy of blue violets, daisies, and apple blossom, it will mean:

Your modesty (violets), and innocence (daisies), secure you the preference (apple blossom).

If your baby was born between the 1st and the 21st of May read pages 22 and 23, but if between the 22nd and the 31st skip to pages 24 and 25.

UNDER
WHAT STARS WAS
MY BABY
BORN?

TAURUS
The Bull
21st April–21st May

GEMINI
The Twins
22nd May–21st June

CANCER
The Crab
22nd June–23rd July

LEO
The Lion
24th July–23rd August

VIRGO
The Virgin
24th August–23rd September

LIBRA
The Scales
24th September–23rd October

SCORPIO
The Scorpion
24th October–22nd November

SAGITTARIUS
The Archer
23rd November–21st December

CAPRICORN
The Sea Goat
22nd December–20th January

AQUARIUS
The Water Bearer
21st January–19th February

PISCES
The Fishes
20th February–20th March

ARIES
The Ram
21st March–20th April

Taurus — the Bull
21st April—21st May

PEOPLE born under Taurus are notable for the quality of endurance. They are patient and tenacious workers, and have exceptionally good memories. No dreamers, they live fully in the external world. In personal relationships they tend to be domineering, and very jealous. Taureans are placid in temperament, slow to anger, but furious when provoked. They incline to ease and luxury, but as an objective for rather than a hindrance to their laboriousness.

For the Taurus Baby

Lucky to wear an emerald.
Lucky stones are malachite, turquoise,
  jade, alabaster.
Lucky metal is copper.
The Taurus baby's colour is green.
Lucky number is 6.
Fortunate day is Friday.

Gemini — the Twins
22nd May–21st June

The distinguishing characteristic of people born under Gemini is intellectual brilliance. They are intuitive as well as observant and are always fond of the arts or sciences. Their understanding of human relationships is swift and sure, though they are apt themselves to be but superficial participants. Gemini people are generally quick and active, even nervous, restless and changeable. They are subtle, perhaps devious. Their conversation is animated, and rich in vocabulary. They need usually to cultivate in their lives a sense of continuity and purpose.

For the Gemini Baby

Lucky to wear topaz, amber, zireen.
Lucky stones are marble, glass.
Lucky metal is quicksilver.
The Gemini baby's colour is yellow.
Lucky number is 5.
Fortunate day is Wednesday.

BABIES BORN
ON
THE SAME DAY
AS
YOUR BABY

IS there any special good fortune in being born on one particular day? Is there any truth in a horoscope — will babies born under Taurus grow up like this, and those born under the sign of Gemini grow up to be like that? Here is a list for you to help you make up your mind whether there is any truth in what the stars foretell.

1st   Joseph Addison, 1672. A. V. Alexander, 1885. General Sir Alan Cunningham, 1887. Danièle Darrieux, 1917. Glenn Ford, 1918.

2nd   Catherine the Great of Russia, 1729. Novalis, 1772. Jerome K. Jerome, 1859. R. E. S. Wyatt, 1901. Bing Crosby, 1904.

3rd   Margaret of Burgundy, 1446. Machiavelli, 1469. D'Oyly Carte, 1844.

Zoltan Korda, 1895. Krishna Menon, 1897.

4th   John James Audubon, 1782. Cardinal Spellman, 1889. Audrey Hepburn, 1929.

5th   Karl Marx, 1818. Sylvia Pankhurst, 1882. Viscount Wavell, 1883. Dr Geoffrey Fisher, Archbishop of Canterbury, 1887. Sir Gordon Richards, 1904. Tyrone Power, 1914.

6th   Pope Innocent X, 1574. Robespierre, 1758. Freud, 1856. Rabindranath Tagore, 1861. Lord Ironside, 1880. Sir Alan Cobham, 1894. Stewart Granger, 1913. Orson Welles, 1915.

7th   Robert Browning, 1812. Brahms, 1833. Tchaikovsky, 1840. A. E. W. Mason, 1865. Gary Cooper, 1901.

8th   Jean Henri Dunant, 1828. Harry S. Truman, 1884. Fernandel, 1903. Roberto Rossellini, 1906.

9th   Sir James Barrie, 1860. Lucy Annie Middleton, 1894.

10th   Sir Thomas Lipton, 1850. Gustav Stresemann 1878. Chief Rabbi Israel Brodie, 1895. Fred Astaire, 1899. Monica Dickens, 1915.

11th   Justinian the Great of Byzantium, 483. Anne of Bohemia, 1366. Irving Berlin, 1888. Paul Nash, 1889. Margaret Rutherford, 1892. Salvador Dali, 1904.

12th   Edward Lear, 1812. Florence Nightingale, 1820. Dante Gabriel Rossetti, 1828. Massenet, 1842. Marquess of Milford Haven, 1919.

13th   Empress Maria Theresa of Hungary and Bohemia, 1717. Pope Innocent XIII, 1655. Pope Pius IX, 1792. Alphonse Daudet, 1840. Sir Arthur Sullivan, 1842. Sir Ronald Ross, 1857. Daphne Du Maurier, 1907.

14th   Margaret of Valois, 1553. Gabriel Daniel Fahrenheit, 1686. Robert Owen, 1771.

15th   Prince von Metternich, 1773. Pierre Curie, 1859. James Mason, 1909.

16th   Pope Innocent XI, 1611. Petrus Cuypers, 1827. Earl of Elgin, 1849. H. E. Bates, 1905. Henry Fonda, 1905. Liberace, 1919. Martine Carol, 1922.

17th   Dr Edward Jenner, 1749. Lord Iliffe, 1877. Princess Arthur of Connaught, 1891. Jean Gabin, 1904. Dennis Brain, 1921.

18th   Czar Nicholas II of Russia, 1868. Bertrand Russell, 1872. Dame Margot Fonteyn, 1919.

19th   Johann Gottlieb Fichte, 1762. Vittorio Emanuele Orlando, 1860. Dame Nellie Melba, 1861. Sir Michael Balcon, 1896.

20th   Balzac, 1799. John Stuart Mill, 1806. Sigrid Undset, 1882. Lord Astor, 1886. David Ormsby Gore, 1918.

21st   Albrecht Dürer, 1471. Philip II of Spain, 1527. Alexander Pope, 1688. Elizabeth Fry, 1780. Joseph Parry, 1841. Le Douanier Rousseau, 1844.

22nd Wagner, 1713. Sir A. Conan Doyle, 1859. Dr Daniel F. Malan, 1874. Sir Laurence Olivier, 1907.

23rd Linnæus, 1707. Mesmer, 1733. Thomas Hood, 1799. Douglas Fairbanks, Sr, 1883. Herbert Marshall, 1890. Sir Hugh Casson, 1910. Barbara Ward, 1914. Denis Compton, 1918.

24th Jean Paul Marat, 1744. Queen Victoria, 1819. Sir Arthur Wing Pinero, 1855. Jan Christian Smuts, 1870. Suzanne Lenglen, 1899. Sir William Haley, 1901.

Joan Hammond, 1912. Mai Zetterling, 1925.

25th   Edward Bulwer-Lytton, 1803. Ralph Waldo Emerson, 1803. Lord Beaverbrook, 1879. Marshal Tito, 1892.

26th   Charles, Duke of Orleans, 1391. Queen Mary, 1867. Sir Eugene Goosens, 1893. George Formby, 1904. John Wayne, 1907. Robert Morley, 1908.

27th   Mrs Bloomer, 1818. Arnold Bennett, 1867. Georges Roualt, 1871. Isadora Duncan, 1878. Sir John Cockcroft, 1897.

28th   George I, 1660. William Pitt the younger, 1759. Thomas Moore, 1779. Dr Edouard Beneš, 1884. Stephen Spender, 1909. Randolph Churchill, 1911.

29th   Charles II, 1630. Sarah, Duchess of Marlborough, 1660. Joseph Fouche, 1763. G. K. Chesterton, 1874. Oswald Spengler, 1880. Beatrice Lillie, 1884. Lord Rothermere, 1898. Bobn Hope, 1904.

30th   Henry IV, 1366. Pierre Janet, 1859. The Duke of Norfolk, 1908. Hugh Griffith, 1912.

31st Walt Whitman, 1819. Pope Pius XI, 1857. Phyllis Bottome, 1884. Peter Fleming, 1907. Edith Coates, 1908. Alida Valli, 1921. Prince Rainier III of Monaco, 1923.

THE UPBRINGING OF MAY BABIES OF THE PAST

AN Earnest Perswasive to all
Mothers (especially those of Rank
and Quality) to Nurse their
own Children.

Consider then, Ladies, what Assurance
you have, that the Mercenary Nurse is not
of a Vicious Disposition, and conclude it
your Duty, not to put off your Child to any
other, unless one from whom it may imbibe
better Qualities than from yourselves. And
since few of those Nicer Dames, who
decline this Office, think better of others
than of themselves, I hope they will not be
so unkind, as to venture their Children
abroad, where they may be likely to draw in
a Disposition to those Vices which they
most abhor. I am much inclined to subscribe

to the Opinion of Wise *Cato,* That for the most part *Noble Matrons are endued with more Vertuous Inclinations* than the meaner sort. And methinks for that reason they ought not to place out their Children with any Women of baser Allay, and less Vertuous Dispositions . . .

Let but a few more truly Generous and Noble Matrons, come in and joyn with those few that have already begun to set this Age a good Example; and such a bright Constellation cannot but be took notice of, and have a vigorous Influence to render it as Fashionable for the future, for Ladies to Discharge this their Duty, as it is as present to Neglect it.

Newcome, *The Complete Mother,* 1695.

This Earnest Perswasive does not seem to have had immediate results, for in *The Times* in the year 1809 this advertisement appears, and such advertisements were common.

WANTS A PLACE

AS *WET-NURSE,* a married Woman, about 24 years of age; she has abundance of milk, and her child is one month old: she can be well recommended. Direct to E. M. No. 13, Little Wild-street, Lincoln's Inn fields.

When I say, be careful of baby, I don't mean have it always in your arms. If the baby is old enough, and the weather warm enough for it to have some heat in itself, it is much better for a child to be crawling about than to be always in its little nurse's arms. And it is much better for it to amuse itself than to have her always making noises to it.

The healthiest, happiest, liveliest, most

beautiful baby I ever saw was the only child of a busy laundress. She washed all day in a room with the door open upon a larger room, where she put the child. It sat or crawled upon the floor all day with no other play-fellow than a kitten, which it used to hug. Its mother kept it beautifully clean, and fed it with perfect regularity. The child was never frightened at anything. The room where it sat was the house-place; and it always gave notice to its mother when anybody came in, not by a cry, but by a crow. I lived for many months

within hearing of that child, and never heard it cry day or night.

I think there is a great deal too much of amusing children now; and not enough of letting them amuse themselves.

Never distract a child's attention. If it is looking at one thing, don't show it another; and so on.

Florence Nightingale, *Notes on Nursing*,
1861.

Under the idea of giving strength to the child's back, and enable it to support itself, it used to be the practice, and still continues in some country villages, to swathe or roll the child very tight round the abdomen, with a very broad roller; by which means the circulation of the blood was impeded, the superior parts loaded, the motion of the intestines, and the action of the abdominal muscles, hindered from properly performing their offices; hence gripes – convulsions – coughs – and general uneasiness. Instead, therefore, of this roller, a short flannel petticoat, with a broad head should be tied on round the waist, only so tight, that a finger will easily pass under it; so that if the child's belly swells, as it sometimes will from flatulence, it may experience no uneasiness: and if after this a long linen gown is put on, the child will be sufficiently dressed, perfectly easy, and no obstruction occur to prevent nature performing her proper operations.

Culpeper, *The Complete English Family Physician*, 1802.

Coral is good to be hanged about children's necks, as well to rub their gums, as to preserve them from the falling sickness.

Plat, *Jewel-House of Art and Nature*, 1594.

CURE FOR RICKETS. — The last time in London I saw the 'operation' for rickets performed by passing a child over the back and under the body of a donkey, was in Hoxton market-place, in May 1845. The operation was thus performed. The mother of the child took the patient in her arms, and began with the odd number 1, whilst the proprietor of the donkey repeated the even number; and thus the poor creature was passed over and under, no other word except the numbers being spoken by either individual.

I saw about twenty or thirty passes, and then grew tired; but I took care to be well informed respecting the method of cure, which was kindly tendered by a spectacled spectator; and for the benefit of the readers of *N. & Q.*, I register it. The passings required are 9 times 9 = 81. No other word must be spoken, and the passing of the child once more or less annuls the efficacy of the operation.

A Correspondent, in *Notes and Queries,*
1855.

The employment of children in manufactories ought not to be looked upon as an evil, till the present moral and domestic habits of the population are completely reorganised. So long as home education is not found for them, and they are left to live as savages, they are to some extent better situated when engaged in light labour, and the labour generally is light which falls to their share. The duration of mill labour, from the natural state of the body during growth, and from its previous want of healthy development, is too long, and masters would do well not to wait for legislation on the subject, but to dismiss their junior hands after eight or ten hours' labour, or it would be still better that they should not commence till eight o'clock, and should terminate at six in the evening.

Gaskell, *The Manufacturing Population*
of England, 1833.

JUVENILE LIBRARY, NO. 41, SKINNER STREET.

This day is published, in 1 vol. 12mo. with a beautiful Frontispiece, by Hopwood, price 3s. 6d. in extra boards.

MRS LEICESTER'S SCHOOL, or, The History of several Young Ladies, related by themselves.

The second edition. 'With much satisfaction do we express our unqualified praise of these elegant and instructive Tales: they are delightfully simple, and exquisitely told. The child or parent who reads the little history of Elizabeth Villiers, will, in spite of any resolution to the contrary, be touched to the heart, if not melted into tears. Morose and crabbed censors as we are represented to be, we closed the volume, wishing there had been another, and lamenting that we had got to the end.' Critical Review for December 1808.

Printed for M. J. Godwin, at the Juvenile Library, 41, Skinner-street, Snowhill; and to be had of all Booksellers.

The Times, 1809.

LEECHES

In applying leeches to children, care should be taken to put them, if possible, over a bone, because we are then enabled by pressure to stop the bleeding from their bites — moderate sized leeches should be chosen — the number must be regulated according to the child's age.

One leech for a child under six months.

Two ditto ditto . . . one year.

Three ditto ditto . . . two years.

Four ditto ditto . . . three years.

While they are drawing, the child should be kept as nearly as can be in a sitting posture, as a more rapid effect is produced upon the system in this position by the abstraction of blood than in a horizontal posture. If the child shews symptoms of faintness the leeches should be removed at once, and the bleeding stopped. In most cases, pressure upon the bites with a little cotton or burnt rag will suffice, but if this be not enough, a finger should be applied upon each bite, and retained with firm pressure against the bone below for several minutes. Should this fail, a drop of Turpentine may be applied to each wound or equal parts of Alum powder and ice. The most powerful mode of arresting the bleeding of leech-bites is the application of caustic, which should be well pressed into the wounds so as to be brought in contact with the whole surface in its deepest part. The leech bites must not, under any circumstance, be allowed to continue bleeding, as children are easily affected by the loss of blood, the young infants have not unfrequently died from the bleeding of a single leech being permitted to continue unchecked for some hours.

Goodeve, *Hints for the General Management of Children in India*, 1844.

There are various opinions as to the propriety of giving children beer. Many do not require it, but thrive sufficiently upon milk. There are others for whom it is heating and heavy;

but there are also some who are thought to need the nourishment it bestows. Mild beer, well hopped, is said to act upon some

constitutions more as a tonic than a stimulant, and to assimilate with animal diet better than any other beverage. We feel some doubt on this point, and would recommend bread and milk, varied by tea and coffee, diluted with milk, as a good breakfast and supper.

Barwell, *Infant Treatment*, 1840.

THREE CUSTOMS

On the calends or first of May, commonly called May-day, the juvenile part of both sexes were wont to rise a little after midnight and walk to some neighbouring wood, accompanied with music and blowing of horns, where they break down branches from the trees, and adorn them with nosegays and crowns of flowers; when this is done, they return with their booty homewards about the rising of the sun, and make their doors and windows to triumph with their flowery spoils; and the after part of the day is chiefly spent in dancing round a tall pole, which is called a May-pole, and being placed in a convenient part of the village, stands there, as it were, consecrated to the Goddess of Flowers, without the least violation being offered to it in the whole circle of the year.

Bourne, *Antiquitates Vulgares*, 1725.

The after part of the day after such a night would be chiefly spent by twentieth century children in sleep.

Athenians, on an early day in spring, every year crowned with flowers all children who had reached their third year, and in this way the parents testified their joy that the little ones had passed the age rendered critical by the maladies incident to infants.

Folkyard, *Plant Lore*, 1884.

FROM THE PARISH BOOKS
OF GATESHEAD

1649. 1 stone of figgs riding the boundarie, 4s. 8d.

Note: These figs were distributed to children, that they might remember the riding of the boundaries. A witness relative to riding the boundaries of Blackburn fell says, that (about 1730) 'the Bishop's Bailiff, Douthwaite, came riding, and sounding a home, and scattered spice and white cakes,' etc. Sometimes the poor bairns were first whipped on the boundary stone, and feasted afterwards.

Surtees, *The History and Antiquities of the County Palatine of Durham,* 1820.

DISTINGUISHED
MAY
BABIES

born May 1780.

This was written by her sister Louisa, then aged 12, which shows the lives of young quakers at that time were not so quiet as is sometimes supposed.

'We went into Norwich. We had blue cockades and I bawled out of the window at a fine rate, 'Gurney for ever' . . . in the evening Scarnel came home and told us that Windham had got the election. I cried. I hated all the aristocrats; I felt it right to hate them. I was fit to kill them.'

Or this also taken from Louisa's diary, gives a picture of the fun the eleven young Gurney children had:

'After breakfast Betsy, Madge, Daisy and I went to the Herrings in the chaise. I never had such a jostling uncomfortable ride. We had a nice little dinner and afterwards went into the garden and picked cherries and plums. At tea officers and gentlemen came in; they were most discourteous and flirtatious. At supper I ate so many brandy cherries that I was half tipsy so Madge and Betsy took me into their room and stuffed some salts and rhubarb down my throat.'

Or this from the same source:

'We have romped most of the morning. In the afternoon we read a novel. In the evening a blind fiddler came and we had a most merry dance.'

Richenda, two years older than Louisa, wrote in her diary:

'Oh, how I long to get a broom and BANG all the old Quakers who do look so disagreeable and cross . . . It was real bliss to hear the clock strike twelve.'

But Elizabeth herself was a thoughtful, serious child, and when she was quite small wrote in her diary:

'A thought passed in my mind that if I had some religion I should be superior to what I am. Can I be really wicked? I may be so . . . If religion be a support why not get it? . . . I don't feel any real religion. I am a fool.'

ALEXANDER POPE
born May 1688.

At the writing of this Ode, he wanted a few days of twelve years of age.

Happy the Man, whose Wish and Care,
  A few paternal Acres bound,
Content to breathe his native Air,
        In his own Ground.

Whose Herds with Milk, whose Fields with Bread,

Whose Flocks supply him with Attire,
   Whose Trees in Summer yield him Shade,
               In Winter, Fire.

Blest, who can unconcern'dly find
   Hours, Days, and Years, slide soft away,
In Health of Body, Peace of Mind,
               Quiet by Day.

Sound Sleep by Night; Study and Ease,
   Together mixt; sweet Recreation,
And Innocence, which most does please,
               With Meditation.

Thus let me live, unseen, unknown,
   Thus, unlamented let me die,
Steal from the World, and not a Stone
               Tell where I lie.

What a poem by somebody not yet twelve !

JOHN BANNISTER
born May 1760.

His entrance on the stage of the world was
distinguished by a comic anecdote, which, in his
latter days, he was used to relate with great glee
and characteristic humour. When the moment

of his birth was approaching, his grandmother, with the superstition of anility, ran to the cupboard for a silver spoon, which she placed between his lips, that he might possess the popular title to good-luck derived from being born with 'a silver spoon in his mouth.'

LINNÆUS
born May 1707.

When the boy was eight years old, a separate plot of ground was assigned him by his father, which was called 'Carl's Garden,' and which he soon stored with collections of plants and wild flowers gathered from woods and fields around his dwelling. At the same time he introduced a variety of weeds; a treasure which it afterwards cost his father no small pains to eradicate from his flower-beds. The enterprising youngster even tried the experiment of establishing a swarm of wild bees and wasps in the garden, the result of which was a devastating warfare waged against the domestic hives.

Brightwell, *A Life of Linnæus*, 1858.

ROBERT OWEN
born May 1771.

I must have been sent young to school, — probably at between four and five years of age, — for I cannot remember first going there. But I recollect being very anxious to be first in school and first home, and the boys had always a race from the school to the town, and, being a fast runner, I was usually at home the first, and almost always the first at school in the morning. On one occasion my haste nearly cost me my life. I used to have for breakfast a basin of flummery, — a food prepared in Wales from flour, and eaten with milk, and which is usually given to children as the Scotch use oatmeal porridge. It is pleasant, and nutritious, and is generally liked by young persons. I requested that this breakfast might be always ready when I returned from school, so that I might eat it speedily, in order to be the first back again to school. One morning, when about five years old, I ran home as usual from school, found my basin of flummery ready, and as I supposed sufficiently cooled for eating, for no heat

appeared to rise from it. It had skinned over as when quite cold; but on my hastily taking a spoonful of it, I found it was quite scalding hot, the body of it retaining all its heat. The consequence was an instant fainting, from the stomach being scalded. In that state I remained so long, that my parents thought life was extinct. However, after a considerable period I revived; but from that day my stomach became incapable of digesting food, except the most simple and in small quantity at a time. This made me attend to the effects of different qualities of food on my changed constitution, and gave me the habit of close observation and of continual reflection; and I have always thought that this accident had a great influence in forming my character.

The Life of Robert Owen, written by
himself, 1857.

JOSEPH ADDISON
born May 1672.

Having, while at a country school in his father's neighbourhood, committed some trifling fault, the dread of punishment or disgrace so affected his imagination as to prompt him to make his escape into the fields and woods, where he is said to have subsisted on fruits, and lodged in a hollow tree, till discovered and brought back to his parents.

Aiken, *The Life of Joseph Addison*, 1843.

THOMAS MOORE
born May 1779.

Immediately after this event, my mother indulged in the strange fancy of having a medal (if such it could be called) struck off, with my name and the date of the birth engraved on it. The medal was, in fact, nothing more than a large crown-piece, which she had caused to be smoothed so as to receive the inscription; and this record of my birth, which, from a weakness on the subject of her children's ages, she had kept always carefully concealed, she herself delivered into my hands when I last saw her, on 16th Feb. 1831; and when she evidently felt we were parting for the last time. For so unusual a mode of commemorating a child's age I can only account by the state of the laws at that period, which, not allowing of the registration of the births of Catholic children, left to parents no other mode of recording them than by some such method as this fondest of mothers devised.

At a very early age I was sent to a school kept by a man of the name of Malone, in the same street where we lived. This wild, odd fellow, of whose cocked hat I have still a very clear remembrance, used to pass the greater part of his nights in drinking at public-houses, and was hardly ever able to make his appearance in the school before noon. He would then generally whip the boys all round for disturbing his slumbers. I was myself, however, a special favourite with him, partly, perhaps, from being the youngest boy in the school, but chiefly, I think, from the plan which then, and ever after, my anxious mother adopted, of heaping with all sorts of kindnesses and attentions, those who were in any way, whether as master, ushers, or schoolfellows, likely to assist me in my learning.

Moore, *Memoirs*, 1853.

MARY GRANVILLE DELANY
born May 1700.

In the year 10 (1710) I first saw Mr Handel,
who was introduced to my uncle Stanley by
Mr Heidegger, the famous manager of the
opera, and the most ugly man that ever was
formed. We had no better instrument in the

house than a little spinnet of mine, on
which that great musician performed
wonders. I was much struck with his playing,

but struck as a child, not a judge, for the moment he was gone, I seated myself to my instrument, and played the best lesson I had then learnt; my uncle archly asked me whether I thought I should ever play as well as Mr Handel. 'If I did not think I should,' cried I, 'I would burn my instrument!' such was the innocent presumption of childish ignorance.

The Autobiography of Mary Granville, Mrs Delany, edited by Lady Llanover, 1861.

JOHN STUART MILL
born May 1806.

I have no remembrance of the time when I began to learn Greek, I have been told that it was when I was three years old. My earliest recollection on the subject, is that of committing to memory what my father termed vocables, being lists of common Greek words, with their signification in English, which he wrote out for me on cards . . .

The only thing besides Greek, that I learnt as a lesson in this part of my childhood, was arithmetic: this also my father taught me: it was the task of the evenings, and I well remember its disagreeableness. But the lessons were only a part of the daily instruction I received. Much of it consisted in the books I read by myself, and my father's discourses to me, chiefly during our walks. From 1810 to the end of 1813 we were living in Newington Green, then an almost rustic neighbourhood. My father's health required considerable and constant exercise, and he walked habitually before breakfast, generally in the green lanes towards Hornsey. In these walks I always accompanied him, and with my earliest recollections of green fields and wild flowers, is mingled that of the account I gave him daily of what I had read the day before. To the best of my remembrance, this was a voluntary rather than a prescribed exercise. I made notes on slips of paper while reading, and from these in the morning walks, I told the story to him; for the books were chiefly histories, of which I read in this manner a great number . . .

J. S. Mill, *Autobiography*, 1873.

GAMES
for the
MAY
BABY

T OUCHING the parts of the baby's
face, say:
Brow, brow, brinkie;
Eye, eye, winkie;
Nose, nose, nopper;
Mouth, mouth, merry;
Cheek, cheek, cherry;
Chin, chin, chopper.

> *Nursery Rhymes, Tales and Jingles,*
> London, 1844.

Light a stick and make it wave rapidly to and
fro, so as to produce a semicircle of red fire
before the child's eyes. The following is a

rhyme appropriate to this fireside phenomenon, which is called a 'dingle dousie.'

Dingle, dingle dousie,
    The cat's at the well;
The dog's awa' to Musselburgh
    To buy the bairn a bell.

Greet, greet, bairnie,
    And ye'll get a bell;
If ye dinna greet, bairnie,
    I'll keep it to mysel'!

Popular Rhymes of Scotland,
W. & R. Chambers, 1842.

DROP THE HANDKERCHIEF. — This game may be played round the may-pole, or without it. The players stand in a circle, holding hands, except one, who carries a handkerchief: he or she runs round and round, and at last throws the handkerchief at the back of one in the circle. That one instantly breaks from the circle, and runs round in an opposite direction to that in which the first was going. Those two between whom he or she was standing, keep their hands apart till one of the two runners is able to enter the circle between them. They then close hands and exclude the last, who has to take the handkerchief, and go on as before. She must continue to run on, throwing the handkerchief until she can get into the circle first.

Kingston, *Infant Amusements*, 1867.

A MAY
CHILD IN
FICTION

ONCE upon a time there was a little chimney-sweep, and his name was Tom. That is a short name, and you have heard it before, so you will not have much trouble in remembering it. He lived in a great town in the North country, where there were plenty of chimneys to sweep, and plenty of money for Tom to earn and his master to spend. He could not read nor write, and did not care to do either; and he never washed himself, for there was no water up the court where he lived. He had never been taught to say his prayers. He never had heard of God, or of Christ, except in words which you never have heard, and which it would have been well if he had never heard. He cried half his time, and laughed the other half. He cried when he had to climb the dark flues, rubbing his poor knees and elbows raw; and when the soot got into his eyes, which it did every day in the week; and when his master beat him, which he did every day in the week; and when he had not enough to eat, which happened every day in the week likewise. And he laughed the other half of the day, when he was tossing halfpennies with the other boys, or playing leap-frog over the posts, or bowling stones at the horses' legs as they trotted by, which last was excellent fun, when there was a wall at hand behind which to hide. As for chimney-sweeping, and being hungry, and being beaten, he took all that for the way of the world, like the rain and snow and thunder, and stood manfully with his back to it till it was over, as his old donkey did to a hail-storm; and then shook his ears and was as jolly as ever; and thought of the fine times coming, when he would be a man, and a master-sweep, and sit in the public-house with a quart of beer and a long pipe, and play cards for silver money, and wear velveteens and ankle-jacks, and keep a white bull-dog with one grey ear, and carry her puppies in his pocket, just like a man.

Charles Kingsley, *The Water-Babies,* 1863.

Here the door opened, and a small quad-room boy, between four and five years of age, entered the room. There was something in his appearance remarkably beautiful and engaging. His black hair, fine as floss silk, hung in glossy curls about his round dimpled face, while a pair of large dark eyes, full of fire and softness, looked out from beneath the rich long lashes as he peered curiously into the apartment. A gay robe of scarlet and yellow plaid, carefully made and neatly fitted, set off to advantage the dark and rich style of his beauty; and a certain comic air of assurance, blended with bashfulness, shewed that he had not been unused to being petted and noticed by his master.

Harriet Beecher Stowe, *Uncle Tom's Cabin*, 1853.

LETTERS
from
ROYAL
MAY
BABIES

74

CHARLES II was born in May 1630. When he was eight years old his mother sent this letter to him:

Charles, I am sorry that I must begin my first letter with chiding you, because I hear that you will not take phisicke. I hope it was onlie for this day, and that tomorrow you will do it; for if you will not, I must come to you and make you take it, for it is for your health. I have given order to mi lord of Newcastel to send mi word to-night whether you will or not; therefore I hope you will not give mi the paines to goe.

    And so I rest
      Your affectionate mother,
        Henriette Marie.

Charles, then, in a letter to his Governor, Lord Newcastle:

My Lord, I would not have you take too much phisicke, for it doth always make me worse, and I think it will doe the like with you. I ride every day, and am ready to follow any directions from you. Make haste back to him that loves you.

Charles, P.

Queen (then Princess) Victoria, aged nine, writing to her Uncle Leopold, later to be King of the Belgians.

My dearest Uncle — I wish you many happy returns of your birthday; I very often think of you, and I hope to see you soon again, for I am very fond of you. I see my Aunt Sophia often, who looks very well, and is very well. I use every day your pretty soup-basin. Is it very warm in Italy? It is so mild here, that I go out every day. Mama is tolerable well and I am quite well.

Your affectionate Niece,

Victoria.

P.S. I am very angry with you, Uncle, for you have never written to me once since you went, and that is a long while.

RHYMES
for the
MAY
BABY

M AY brings flocks of pretty
lambs,
Sporting round their fleecy dams.
Sara Coleridge (1802–1852).

INCIDENTS IN THE LIFE OF MY UNCLE ARLY

I

O My agèd Uncle Arly !
Sitting on a heap of Barley
   Thro' the silent hours of night, –
Close beside a leafy thicket: –
On his nose there was a Cricket, –
In his hat a Railway-Ticket; –
   (But his shoes were far too tight.)

II

Long ago, in youth, he squander'd
All his goods away, and wander'd
   To the Tiniskoop-hills afar.
There on golden sunsets blazing,
Every evening found him gazing, –
Singing, –'orb! you're quite amazing!
   How I wonder what you are!'

III

Like the ancient Medes and Persians,
Always by his own exertions
  He subsisted on those hills; –
Whiles, – by teaching children spelling, –
Or at times by merely yelling, –
Or at intervals by selling
  Propter's Nicodemus Pills.

IV

Later, in his morning rambles
He perceived the moving brambles –
  Something square and white disclose; –
'Twas a First-class Railway-Ticket;
But, on stooping down to pick it

Off the ground, — a pea-green Cricket
    Settled on my uncle's Nose.

V

Never — never more, — oh! never,
Did that Cricket leave him ever, —
    Dawn or evening, day or night; —
Clinging as a constant treasure, —
Chirping with a cheerious measure, —
Wholly to my uncle's pleasure, —
    (Though his shoes were far too tight.)

VI

So for three-and-forty winters,
Till his shoes were worn to splinters,
    All these hills he wander'd o'er, —
Sometimes silent, — sometimes yelling; —
    Till he came to Borley-Melling,
Near his old ancestral dwelling; —
    (But his shoes were far too tight.)

VII

On a little heap of Barley
Died my aged uncle Arly,
    And they buried him one night; —
Close beside the leafy thicket; —

There, – his hat and Railway-Ticket; –
There, – his ever-faithful Cricket; –
  (But his shoes were far too tight.)
            Edward Lear (1812–1888).

O can ye sew cushions,
    Can ye sew sheets,
Can ye sing, Ba-loo-loo,
    When the bairnie greets?

And hee and ba, birdie,
    And hee and ba, lamb;
And hee and ba, birdie,
    My bonnie lamb!

Hee O, wee O,
    What wad I do wi' you?

Black is the life
    That I lead wi' you.
Ower mony o' you,
    Little for to gie you;
Hee O, wee O,
    What wad I do wi' you?
         Popular Rhymes of Scotland,
        W. & R. Chambers, 1842.

A PRAYER

To-night I lie me down to sleep,
I pray the Lord my soul to keep;
If I should die before I wake,
I pray the Lord my soul to take.
   Our Children, by Mrs Wood, 1876.

GOODNIGHT
to the
MAY
BABY

NOW that the evenings stay light so late, you have perhaps your curtain undrawn and are looking at the galaxy of stars that fill the May sky. As you look you are of course thinking of your baby. Is a fate written for it in the sky, if only you could read it? And suppose you could read it, would you wish to interfere, and to change this gift for that? Perhaps, for it is hard not to wish for a baby those qualities and gifts you would most have liked for yourself: you are seeing a Fonteyn riding the Great Bear, or a prime minister on Cassiopeia. But if you are, it is almost certain before you go to sleep you will have given up such dreams. For your own childhood will have taught you that no amount of wishful thinking by parents changes the child. And what a good thing, for surely to your baby you will say, 'Darling, I wouldn't change you. I like you exactly as you are.'

Noel Streatfeild